Baldy

Poems by

Cameron Morse

Kansas City   Spartan Press   Missouri

Spartan Press
Kansas City, MO
spartanpresskc.com

Copyright © Cameron Morse, 2020
First Edition 1 3 5 7 9 10 8 6 4 2
ISBN: 978-1-950380-87-9
LCCN: 2020931252

Design, edits and layout: Jason Ryberg
Cover image: Lauren Emmons
Author photo: Brian Compton
All rights reserved. No part of this publication may be reproduced or transmitted in any form or by any means, electronic or mechanical, including photocopying, recording or by info retrieval system, without prior written permission from the author.

Thanks to my wife Lili, my son Theodore Ian and daughter Naomi Mira along with my parents and siblings Jessie, Mariah and Cory. Our life together provides the inspiration and basis of lived experience for these poems. Another debt is owed to the members of the GBM SURVIVORS TO THIVERS! Facebook group for their stories; L.S. Klatt, my first mentor; the Creative Writing Program at the University of Missouri—Kansas City; Jason Ryberg, for adopting me into the Spartan family; Jordan Stempleman, for opening up my mind and challenging me aesthetically; the Copyright Agency's Cultural Fund for their Best Poetry Award; Jack Grapes Poetry Prize judge F. Douglas Brown for selecting "Night Clouds in the Black Hills" and the editors in whose magazines the following poems first appeared (in various forms):

8 Poems: "El Maguey." *Adelaide Literary Magazine:* "Warning Label." *Aeolian Harp Anthology:* "Becoming a Father." *Alba:* "Cheese Grater," "Flyswatters," "Dadgum." *Arcturus Magazine:* "Paradise." *Bending Genres:* "Disposable Dogs." *The Big Windows Review:* "IKEA." *The Blue Moon Literary & Art Review:* "Cravings," "The Steamin' Bean." *Communion Arts Journal:* "Looking for God," "Birding on a Sunday Morning." *The Conglomerate:* "Coat Hook." *CULTURAL WEEKLY:* "Night Cloud in the Black Hills." *CutBank:* "Yellow Sac Spider." *Evening Street Review:* "White Petals." *Former People:* "Crocs," "Seven Years." *The Gravity of the Thing:* "Kiddie Pool Baptismal." *Guttural Magazine:* "Letter to an Unknown Sender." *HERON TREE:* "Visitation." *I-70 Review:* "A Vision of My Father." *The Indianapolis Review:* "End-of-Life Scenario." *indicia:* "Striptease." *Lullwater Review:* "Stay-at-Home Dad." *Magnolia Review:* "Flying Snail," "Father's Day." *Meniscus Literary Journal:* "Newborn Panorama." *Metaworker LitMag:* "The Juicer." *Midwest Quarterly:* "Going to the Mayo Clinic." *MockingHeart Review:* "Yellow Curry." *Off the Coast:* "Wild Oats." *The Other Journal:* "What's Still." *Plainsongs:* "Buried Fragrances." *Portland Review:* "The Pourer." *Queen Mob's Teahouse:* "Shave Gel." *Rogue Agent:* "Chiefs Cap." *Route 7 Review:* "Walmart Supercenter," "The Parrot," "Instructions for Coarsening," "Sound Puzzle," "Apple Cider Vinegar." *Shot Glass Journal:* "June 8, Still Spring."*Sprung Formal:* "Dinner Bell Café," "The Oneironaut." *Squawk Back:* "Older Brother," "New Member." *Third Wednesday:* "Down the Road." *Touchstone:* "Aloe Vera." *Unearthed:* "Python," "Dreaming of Yantai." *Verse-Virtual:* "Loadmasters," "Memory Gaps." *Whale Road Review:* "Perceiving Mystery."

TABLE OF CONTENTS

Invocation of a Black Orb-Weaver / 1

mystery

Yellow Sac Spider / 5

Dinner Bell Café / 7

Night Clouds in the Black Hills / 8

A Vision of My Father / 9

Perceiving Mystery / 10

El Maguey / 11

Walmart Supercenter / 12

Dadgum / 14

Disposable Dogs / 15

Python / 16

Older Brother / 17

Visitation / 18

Looking for God / 19

New Member / 20

Letter to an Unknown Sender / 21

Birding on a Sunday Morning / 22

What's Still / 24

End-of-Life Scenario / 25

danger

Becoming a Father / 29

Kiddie Pool Baptismal / 30

Yellow Curry / 32

Buried Fragrances / 33

The Pourer / 34

Striptease / 35

Warning Label / 36

Flyswatters / 37

The Parrot / 38

Cheese Grater / 39

The Juicer / 40

Flying Snail / 41

Loadmasters / 42

Shave Gel / 43

Stay-at-Home Dad / 44

Dreaming of Yantai / 45

Crocs / 46

Sound Puzzle / 47

desire

Newborn Panorama / 51

Chiefs Cap / 53

June 8, Still Spring / 54

Down the Road / 55

Wild Oats / 56

The Oneironaut / 57

Seven Years / 58

Father's Day / 59

Aloe Vera / 60

Instructions for Coarsening / 61

Cravings / 62

Memory Gaps / 64

The Steamin' Bean / 65

IKEA / 66

White Petals / 67

Paradise / 69

Going to the Mayo Clinic / 70

Coat Hook / 71

Apple Cider Vinegar / 72

for poets, the parents of poets, poet parents.

Invocation of a Black Orb-Weaver

Is that you, Bashō,
is that your horned abdomen
plastered to the lineated hillock
of my Moleskine? After falling
into the arms of an overgrown
Rose of Sharon, brandishing
blank pages, I have to know.
Am I not assiduous, assiduous
in the pursuit of my aim, your aim,
who can tell the difference anymore,
black orb-weaver, between your heart
and mine? Both bleed. Both muddy
the silence, the virginal blankness
of being. Suppose you caught me
instead of I you, and ensnared me
in roses, could I not then say
I have become the poem?

mystery

Yellow Sac Spider

One morning I find on the kitchen counter a torn piece of a paper towel with the word *spider* in green highlighter resting atop my empty jar of Barilla pesto, unscrew the cap and walk the partially rinsed jar to the flowerbed, army green flecks of basil still slicked to the glass. A yellow sac spider, indeed, lay at the bottom of the translucent rink. Who left the name of its species, any of the predaceous arachnids of the order Araneae, I can only infer from the neatness of the script to have been my mother. With whom my wife and I have lived all these years since the year of my first seizure and subsequent treatments for brain cancer. I can only guess *my* spider—for upon my reception of this missive it became mine or at least mine to dispose of—crawled into the jar of its own volition only to be discovered there by Mom because she has in her life squashed her fair share of spiders and would not have hesitated to expunge another, especially one caught trespassing on the immaculate quartz countertop. For my part, understanding how arachnophobia is presumed to be genetically hardwired due to troubled prehistorical relations between us and them, I prefer to extend pardon and proffer a life unfettered among phloxes. I set the jar down and walk away as I once dropped two pet turtles in a campus pond because I was tired of them and breaking up with the girl with whom I'd carried back the terrarium from a wet market to my sixth-floor apartment at the Shandong Institute of Business and Technology, the girl I could never be gone from, who later became my wife.

A week or so has elapsed since I returned my tallow
little friend to what constitutes for eight barbed legs and
miniscule brain the wild or at least a more natural habitat
than a six-ounce jar of various ingredients including but not
limited to grana Padano cheese, potato flakes, and cultured
milk, salt, enzymes. Deciding it may be time to pay a visit,
I step out into the stillness and heat and intermittent breeze
of mid-April sun rising at the birding hour of morning to
find alas the poor soldier in the same position as the one
in which I first made his acquaintance, the legs alongside
one half of his abdomen twirled together, the other half's
legs splayed. Everything for naught, the note, the period
of captivity, the release to the wild, all of it: the return visit
from Beijing, family vacation to Florissant in which I fell
as if seized by lightning and convulsed at the foot of the
wardrobe, the ambulance ride butt cracks of EMTs moth
beating at the headlamp CAT scan and subsequent MRI,
all of it for a drowned sailor, a disembodied member of a
species generally hated by members of my own and maybe
even murdered by my own mother. What joy is this, devoid
of content, what empty joy.

Dinner Bell Café

In Eagleville, Missouri, where my parents split cinnamon rolls as Graceland undergrads, I order a veggie omelet with cottage cheese. In the Chapel upstairs, a lamplit broom closet complete with an altar rail and Holy Bible splayed among sermons on cassette or CD, a stand of tracts *FREE FOR OUR TRUCKER FRIENDS*, Lili breastfeeds. Outside, slot machines sport manga girls in string bikinis, coinless plastic buckets tossed at cartoon feet, empty cups, empty hours, showers behind locked doors. The lounge coffee table holds an ashtray and TV remote. My son suckles in the blood light of the chapel. Semis idle at the pump, stalled, waiting for drivers. When the pigtailed waitress comes back, I imagine her a trucker's wife, her life flipped into a ditch like her husband's livelihood in the blizzard I weathered to arrive at my father's sperm, my mother's egg.

Night Clouds in the Black Hills

Thunder crashes like a chest of drawers
pushed down a flight of stairs
in anger, intimations of divorce.
Light leaks out of crevasses between the toes

of clouds. I watch the darker form of some
clouds caterpillar across the lighter
form of others. The pines blacken
in my window screen. Silent lightning flickers like a dying

lightbulb in the darkest corner of the sky.
I know this is paltry and predictable. Treefrogs trill.
I am still. For a long time, I listen to the sound of water
rushing somewhere down below,

water or wind. Who can tell the difference?
Clouds calve like glaciers above the dark chimney:
Clouds colliding with clouds,
clouds within clouds, a catastrophe within me.

A Vision of My Father

After dragging the door
to the side yard—the three pickets
that used to swing
between chain link and cedar sections
of the fence—I can feel
the chalky weather on my hands.

No difference between the smudge
on the hem of my T-shirt
and the light that dapples the boards.
Even T.S. Eliot and I must have
had something in common.
Even in bitten leaves, a blue sky glows.
A blue sky glows in the bitemarks.

Last night I had a vision of my father
in his Panama, gray T-shirt tucked
into his shorts, stretched over his paunch.
Long socks and short shorts.
I lay down my head and had a vision.

A crab apple pops off the garden door
my brother Cory and I unhinged,
just the two of us, one of the cast-iron
flaps uplifted, the other downcast
in tall grass. A crab apple pops
off the mossy picket, its snap
the fingers of a hypnotist.

Perceiving Mystery

Empty of desire, perceive mystery.
  Filled with desire, perceive manifestations.
    —Lao-Tzu

Rusty spade, empty bird bath,
bowl of water filled for the dogs, emptied
for the birds, laundry tossed
in the nostril of the exhaust fan. For months,
I feel nothing. Write nothing
but prose. My father speaks of an underlying
mystery. How did I end up here?

Frost bites. Dead skin flakes.
A white blister crowns my thumb. I used to run
naked in the blizzard
of my desire. Now I sit with arms full
of my son. Mother's rake rasps
in the flower garden. Yesterday's coffee filter
flops in the trash, still seeping.

I hear you talking from a great distance.
You are not the woman I married. Naming,
you are the mother of ten thousand things.
You call them *crocuses*. Green tongues
parting oak leaves to lick my hand.
Sparrows, those black brown stirrings
in the wisteria vine. You call me Husband,
Father. You call me Son.

El Maguey

A little boy I bury my face
in the pillow after Mom confronts me
in the corridor with a newspaper
clipping, an ad for brassieres she discovers
in my jeans. Ashamed as if for the first
time and for all time thereafter,
I will never live it down. I drown
myself in shame. Smother my mouth.
Now she and Mariah accuse my 17-year-old
brother of peeking through his fingers
and make him leave the family room
during an episode of *Endeavour.* I overhear
his older sister say it's just better
if you use a pillow. Some time after my nightmare
in the bedroom, Dad over tacos at El Maguey
states enigmatically that thinking leads
to doing and leaves it at that.
He's long left the family.

Walmart Supercenter

Mom takes my arm in the Walmart
parking lot, walking along
the slanted column of cars in early

winter dark toward a distant spot
into which she slid her RAV4, parking far
enough to silence the inner worrywart.

A seer of wanton doors kicked open
or flung, runaway shopping carts,
a note not even tucked below

her windshield wiper, Mom takes
my arm, my father gone,
filing for divorce in Guam,

for no undivided property, that insidious
double negative betraying
a desire to halve her homestead,

scatter her nestlings. Mom takes
my arm and tells me a client
came in recently who heard the pop,

pop, pop! of gunshots where we
were just digging through a bin of DVDs,
perusing bottles of body wash.

Angels in lime-green vests ushered her into a back
room to wait the twenty minutes
it took the police to arrive.

Dadgum

Dad gone
during a game of peek-a-boo
disappeared
behind his own hands.

Disposable Dogs

What haunts me is how easily conversation
flows through end-of-life scenarios
to the next pet the winter morning our ten-year-old
golden spaniel mix
has what appears to be a heart attack.

Afterwards, my little sister Mariah's key won't ignite
the engine of her Hyundai Accent.
We gather in the driveway. She holds the copper
jaws apart, one in each hand,
and clamps plus to plus, negative to negative.

Not to be late for work, she pulls out of the driveway.

When I see him stretch his neck toward heaven the way
my wife gulps pills and convulse, Mom drops
her scrambled eggs and bacon at the butcher's block
and spills into the back yard to cradle his sinking head.
I leave my oil-splashed plate's quiche in shambles,
go to her. He watches us watch him quiver.

What haunts me is the speed, how swiftly
after one leaves, the next arrives to fill the vacancy.
What haunts me is the vacancy.

Python

No one told me how long I had to live.
No one quoted the statistics.
Even the python in Mom's dream

was dead, lying on the dining room table
during a Morse family gathering.
No one prophesied the amount of time left

in my ledger. I raise my eyes.
There is no more snow on the ground.
I raise my eyes. Juniper shadows

waggle their dark tongues, air warm
as the inside of a mouth. I draw in
close enough to hear the crackle

of snowmelt. Ice unclenches its fist.
Slush squashes under my heel. Little ice
castles sink into the softening green.

Older Brother

If I step outside to scrape burnt bacon and egg over a bowl of dog food and sense a childhood ghost squatting in my periphery above an oak leaf, I, too, might think twice about saying hello, especially when only he and I are home. I would find his behavior strange, far be it from me to speculate on the particular properties of the leaf, the frost glittering on the spine, say, or serrating its edges. Nor would I pay him any mind if my ghost follows the dogs as they go about their day, patrolling the pickets or sprinting into a flurry of barks at the passing of a jogger beyond them. Why should I greet him? He seems more interested in the patio's dark tributaries of dog water spilled perhaps by me, perhaps by accident, than in forming a connection with one of the living. To me my older brother died a long time ago. Why does he linger on, like smoke in the kitchen, long after I've finished breakfast? Why does he push in my captain's chair after I've gone upstairs to take a shower?

Visitation

I am sitting in the driveway
waiting for the scent, the hint of what direction
you might have taken. The shadow of a chicken hawk
splashes my periphery. What now?

When my visitor perches in the sprawling empty branches of God
knows what tree across the circle? As if to say, *describe me,*
my white-speckled breast, my magnificent wingspan
outstretched as I swoop high and float above the ground.

Caught, I cannot argue. I am not a proud head turning aquiline
profile, perusing fallen leaves for trembling
morsels of meat. I'm not even a healthy representative
of my own species.

Still, I rise to receive you. For a long time,
you ignore me. And then you leave.

Looking for God

We're going to the back yard to look for God, I say. Double-layer your legs and zip up your hood. We're going to look for God in the cold wind. We're going to hang out with the dogs.

After I leash the rowdy one to the swing set, you stray within his reach. He leaps you down in patches of snow. He goes in for a kiss with his wet snout. I brush off the crystals caking your rear end, airlift and release you elsewhere.

We're going to look for God elsewhere.

Nevertheless, the icicled swings lure and ensnare. Wind gnaws our noses, your cheeks furnaced red from within. The paws tip you over again into seashell shards of ice.

We're going to look for God in the ice, I suggest, cracked sheets of ice on the back patio. Stay away from the dogs.

New Member

Welcome to the world turned upside down, as you so eloquently put it, four weeks ago when you woke to something wrong to say the least. I, too, am GBM. Going on five years now, I wake to the last of the snowmelt. The head of my shovel cradles clear water. Last night I dreamt of an experimental new therapy, leaned back in a swivel chair baby bird agape and waited for a single drop of clear liquid to be placed on my tongue. Before you woke, four weeks ago, you may not have considered death a real possibility. Now bruised arms and steroids are your reality. You feel weird because of the steroids. Your face is bloated and your heart burns despite the proton-pump inhibitors. Four weeks ago, I walked out my year-old into bright snow light. This morning I woke to the curbside's last shrinking pile, a dead polar bear, oak leaves caught in its bedraggled fur.

Letter to an Unknown Sender

After diagnosis a cloud of unknowing settles
in the air around you, patient,
a mist you breathe in, a prickle of particles
on the tongue, the terrible ambiguity

of what's arrived. It feels like rain
because she said it would
rain this morning over breakfast, eggs
scrambled with hemp seeds and blueberries.

It feels like rain in the driveway
where my year-old totters
in glow-in-the-dark tennis shoes,
fetches a mushroom figurine
from the leaf-quilted flowerbed and drops it.
In slow-motion, the saucer shatters.

He raises the broken stem to his lips.

How close we come to that which cannot be
unlearnt, stumbling over the garden hose
as wind rakes the sere garland
of leaves above. I can only catch so much.

His ceaseless oral exploration of the outside
world continues. Its corners and edges
teach hard lessons. I grip his wrist.
shake the pottery shards from his hand.

Birding on a Sunday Morning

Sunday morning too April
bright in rising sun to know a grackle

from a robin, dark silhouettes
plunge beak first into the plush, shoulders

pumping. Bird shapes surface
swinging earthworms and snap in half

the tender segments, tidbits
from the underground. Sunday morning

too April bright to know an acorn
from a scarab, I swear I see a grackle

choking down the hatted seed, yellow
meth head eyeball fastened upon me,

iridescent coat too motor oil slick
for a starling. Starlings are like

19th century surgeons in black waistcoats.
They're here, too. Holding wings

like hands behind the back, the starlings
pace the bright stage

of the side yard, dipping the golden
sewing needles of their beaks

into the grass, the streetlight's long
incision. Sunday morning

I stay home. I want God the way
I want you. I want Him

for myself. No one else can know.

What's Still

Rain dusts the air
so faintly it can only be seen
crossing the dark leaves
of the ornamental pear.
With what's still and what's
moving in the seam
of mud between sidewalk and side
yard, I take my seat.
One white maggot inches in the dark
gash like the fingertip
of an infant. An entire congregation
lies still around it. I feel the tingle
of rain like a collar of cobweb
on the nape of my neck.
Whatever God I'm after, the worm
lord or child born, I doubt
I'll find Him here in baby flies.
Nevertheless, I am here, I am
here still, I am still.

End-of-Life Scenario

Beyond the turmoil of the day-to-day, tumor
inoperably couch-potatoed

in my brain, a puma
sprung to pounce, I know a seat

for me is waiting. It waits to receive the weight
of my body, a seat at the helm

of the invisible
spaceship that will take me

back to the beginning, the cradle
that rocks the patient into that state

of permanent vergetablehood
into which I know, one day,

he must slip, as if head-thwacked
in the bathtub.

It's not a rocking chair,
per se, not exactly, but it will rock him in dappled

shade tinkling wind chimes: the songs of birds
whose names he never learned.

danger

Becoming a Father

I didn't become a father the moment he was born,
or a husband the moment I married. No,
when I lifted him screaming in my ear
onto the changing table and our arms locked,
I became a father. When I reached around
for the tab and jabbed my forefinger
into the ooze of orange, seedy feces,
then lifted the unbuttoned flap of his onesie
away from the buildup without breaking down,
I became, I triumphed in what I was,
what I would have found unimaginable as a boy:
one steely being born out of duty into the service of another,
a son, an obstinately taciturn word made flesh,
some kind of homunculus with ideas all his own.

Kiddie Pool Baptismal

My feet dunked, I float
my Crocs, nurse

the spilt in my head
with trips to the spigot.

Heal me, sweet
mother, if you think

I'm worth it. Bless
the inventor

of water and one more
way to withstand

the summer. Jungle cat
rugs of heat

piled plush on my chest,
I pluck off my T-shirt,

squeeze rainbows
out of a spray-bottle.

Theo empties cups
over my kneecaps, raising

the dark waterline
of soaked denim. The more

I resist the pastoral, the greater
my urge is to pastor.

Yellow Curry

Theo raises the bowl in both hands.
A mudslide of ground beef and bell pepper
buries the lower half of his face.
Yellow pellets of lawn fertilizer speckle

the driveway, pearls of pesticide
embedded in the side yard. I trace the trajectory
of turmeric from the whipped spoon
to the pastel wall behind his booster seat.

Somewhere a bird calls. I recognize the shriek
of a blue jay. Another sounds out the u
in *you, you, you*—the vowel in *pew*,
the bench Lili sits on at the butcher block.

Napkins clump below her mopping hand.
Theo swings in wide arcs. His hands streak
the varnished surface of the pond.
Trucks and sedans breeze along Duncan Road.

Things are near and far away. A glob of sauce
dangles from Theo's chin. Sun suffuses
light among the clouds. Ramshackle packs
of leaves scamper across the cul-de-sac.

Buried Fragrances

A bumblebee climbs
unkempt stalks of catmint along the front steps,
swooping between the purple bells.

Burying its face in fragrance, the bee is
oblivious. I could stand here a thousand years.
It would never lift its head.

The Pourer

He wants me not
to push his swing but swing
beside him. It requires a kind of
maternal patience to fill
the earthenware pourer with olive oil
the way my mother does: Easing
the jug in both arms, Grandma tilts
until the golden syrup can fall
through the air toward a small black
opening, not knowing until it brims
how much longer she must hold
still, staring into the hole, with the weight
of the bottle aching in her arms.
After writing a longwinded email
to Professor Klatt, I step outside to pace
the sidewalk, barefoot in the driveway,
and ruminate. I hold
my son's feet, rotate and massage his
21-month-old ankles, lick my
thumbnail and scrape smudges of avocado
on his cheek, his temple, the fleck
of cheddar on his chin.

Striptease

A centipede retracts into the mopboard.
I dab it with toilet paper, its furrowed little brow.
My boy screams all morning. Snot dribbles
over his lips. Already disheveled magnolia blossoms
wobble in the wind. One's crumpled.
Another's creased. Still more fuzzy green calyces
have yet to peel back all the way
their lavender petals, baring white inner thighs.

As the sun rises, shadow slides down
the widow's peak of the house. Earlier I spotted
a troop of grackles among the grass, beautiful
intruders long departed. Here there will always be
house sparrows in the bird houses that float
among tendrils in the rafters of the wisteria arbor.

There will always be family. An American robin
jabs at earthworms. Late morning blossoms
catch flame. Theo squints, swinging through shadow
and light in the large timber sawhorse
of the swing set. He holds to his chest the floppy
sunhat Lili bought to shade his head. I kick the empty
dog food bowl and shout *GET SOME!*

Warning Label

I know my mouth is open.
I would like to close my burning
eyes in the heatstroke sun
of the first of July. But the yellow
snail kiddie pool describes
how children drown, one by one,
in language after language.

Three dusty lawn chairs surround me.
Theo carries an orange cup.
When the idea of a refill strikes him,
he grunts at the spigot, begins
to cry then comes to fetch water
from inflatable rubber lining
of the snail. I try to think
of all the things I've heard said,
or read, and what might not
yet have been written. In tree shade,

the pendulum of his child swing
veers right as if S-hooked
a link shorter on that side, his neck
flopped right. His ballcap drops.
Uh-oh, he says. One of the first words
he learned, he learned from me.

Flyswatters

Killing a fly requires too much
patience when all you want
is my flyswatter, not your flyswatter,
not the one I wash for you.

You're not even two and I'm afraid
of you because you walk on
down the lane as if we didn't have to get back
in time for breakfast.

The Parrot

Among Minyon's lawn
ornaments, a parrot swivels
in a copper ring. Its back
is always to me, its hunched
shoulders. Theo carries a bouquet
of silver forks: My son runs
amuck with the toothbrush in his mouth
the way I poked a flap in pink skin
with the Wendy's straw once
and my mouth welled with blood.
The parrot's head hangs chest
low as if necked, as if brooding
upon its own demise. Flies
terrorize me, sponging off my mug
of morning coffee. Breezes nudge
the demon, bestowing glimpses
of its dark beak, a meat hook
buried in particolored plumage.

Cheese Grater

You pick up shreds
from the block

I'm shredding.
You sit on my lap and pick

at the plate, the table,
the grate, and when

the waxy yellow brick
crumbles down to one final

clump I can't grate
without grating

my fingertips,
you pick up that as well.

The Juicer

In the dream, I'm falling.
I tell you I'm falling. One arm
hooked onto the ice shelf, the other
wrapped about my boy, I fall
into the dark Arctic river.

In the morning Mariah plunges
down on the food pusher. She drops
a cucumber into the roaring
hole and out trickles green. After I drop,

my dream screen cuts
to you, back in our apartment,
looking for your shoes
among extended family members.
Mariah drops in a carrot.

Out drips orange. Theo waves
goodbye and closes the closet door
in a game where I pretend
to forget he's in there. The surprise
of it is the storm door

locks itself and me out
of the house: Theo alone, at 22 months,
is in it. I still don't believe he could
have reached the latch.

Flying Snail

Dark rain has lifted the yellow snail kiddie pool
from its perch on the swing set platform
and hurtled it into the farthest-flung
corner of the yard. It's fun to imagine
the snail's buck-toothed, goofy grin
the moment it slams into cedar.

Fun to imagine the sky throwing its dark
tantrum overhead, and what if
the branch-snapping air had slipped
a finger under the rubber dish and flipped it
over the pickets onto Duncan Road
and a Ford F-150 had swerved

away from the blurry yellow form ahead
into a station wagon
full of children's songs like *Where Is
Thumbkin* or some such mayhem
and the snail's smile could not
have melted because decals are permanent?

Far from the hilarity of that, the small pool
traveled only a few paces
before the weight of rain gathering
in its inflatable rubber lining
slowed the mucus slider to a crawl.

Loadmasters

After the boy finishes
his oatmeal, I let the dog in
to lick the floor. Encrusted
with the goop of milky
oats and chia seeds, Theo squirms
in his booster seat. I pass him
pecans from my own plate,
forking the last bites of quiche
into my mouth, a tactic
that allows me time to finish
as Theo leans over the arm
of the captain's chair and spits
bits of masticated pecan
onto the floor and Sherlock's paws
clickety-clack to lick
the same tiles a second time.
At the corner of Birch and Golfview,
I hold Theo's wrist, his hand
loaded with sticks, pulled
weeds, fallen leaves. Garbage
trucks lumber up one lane
and down the other, hiss and swivel
around us. Their grilles tower
over my head, their bumpers over his.

Shave Gel

Theo says *Mama* and hands me
a hair from your head so long its ends
twirl together. Today is
the bottle of my shave gel
he won't let go of as if it contained
some wish-granter and his wish
were to replace me forever
in an equation of Mommy and me.

He crawls into the family
room crate, corning Sherlock,
and pulls shut the door behind him.
Pull the plume and he
discovers shed hair sticks between fingers,
dog hair and cobwebs,
all the ephemera of having a baby

cricket in your afternoon's
last mouthful of ice coffee. I could see my boy
stabbing the tolerant,
sad-eyed cockapoo out of sheer curiosity
but for the distraction
of a garbage truck, salvation from the tedium
of homestay parenting, parenting
home, I stay at home.

My life is an unanswered question
and every day I ask again.

Stay-at-Home Dad

Little canopies of spider
web collect water, spangling globules.
Ed hands down the ceiling fan from a stepladder
blade by blade, layer after layer.

I touch the utility lighter to the tip of the wick,
thumb the copper head
and the garden hose explodes
into spray. I'm coming to terms with the term

stay-at-home dad. Arcing the words over chicken
wire, I'm watering the maple seedling
to which Grandma would prefer any other tree.
In the laundry room, string beans roll out

of the dirty folds of Theodore's dinosaur
onesie: severed fingers, witch-green.
Out walking, he trips in silt and shatters
the wheel of his toy truck. One by one,

his vehicles succumb to love and fascination.
I had only to transplant the shoot
from a flowerbed a few yards away.
For some reason, I water it every day.

Dreaming of Yantai

Magnolia mostly done now, or undone,
more finished than forthcoming, I dream
of Yantai where the stairwell scrunches
until it's like I'm spelunking, scooting
on my butt toward the exit.

Theo bounds into the green in his green
alligator jacket from Beijing. Rows of cut grass
from Grandma's morning ride around. I dab
the droplet of milk on his chin
with the bib. Sherlock swishes the white plume

of his tail at the back door. I dream of you,
belly sagging from childbirth,
who were so young. I miss class because I'm in Yantai,
I miss classes I'm enrolled in, entire programs
of study. As waterworks supervisor,

I oversee the splatter and splotch. Sherlock lifts
a hind leg to the elephant grass.
Theo pours his cup into the dog food bowl, launching
a miniature fleet of brown floaties, captain
of kernels, soggy cereal.

Crocs

I start putting mixed nuts into my mouth
until I remember what I'm here for. A gray squirrel
curls its tail into a question mark. I don't know
how it must feel to put my fingers through the holes
on my Crocs. Why don't you remove your hospital
teat and tell me, Captain Soggy Cereal, why
don't you empty your own Contigo over dog food?
Memory's a container too hot out of the washing
machine, too cold out of the freezer.
Lili bought me Crocs because my feet were hot.
It was July in New York City and no one expected me to live.
I ripped off my socks under the table. Then,
and there. A little black girl rings the doorbell, bag full
of the blond Jesus. Stops at the car parked curb
and sighs before proceeding up the drive.

Sound Puzzle

No one expects a board puzzle to scream at you,
no matter how many firetrucks
it has, so I'm completely sympathetic
when Theodore wails along with the sound box.
I hold him and rub his back, seat
him on my lap and try again with the insidious
toy Melissa & Doug thought

would be a not half-bad idea. Before bed,
Lili and I Velcro crib rail covers to the crib rail.
We didn't want paint in his mouth was
how it started. Now it's part of the procedure
for him to rip off the bedtime prophylactics.

We listen at the basement door: Theo binklieless now
vocalizes among the whitewashed bars.
The nightlight glowing in the kitchenette spreads
a watery stain on the countertop. *Yeah*,
he seems to sing. Moments before, he'd been shrieking.

I wake up with a bite on the back of a doughy hand.
I don't feel like myself, fatigued somehow,
somnolent, far from the presence of God. *Ah*,
he croons, like here I am, all alone again.
Yeah, it's dark but I'm OK. I'm alone but I'm safe.

desire

Newborn Panorama

Winner of Copyright Agency's Cultural Fund Best Poetry Award

Day of first abdominal ultrasound
my firstborn trawls concrete with his blankie
catching catkins and maple seed
helicopter pods. This you called my mortal
panorama, this boy climbing the patio table grate,
these dogs pissing the arbor vitae brown, burnt
orange, until Ed raises the chicken wire a couple of heads
taller the day of her first abdominal ultrasound.
Theo observes the absence of the swing I unhinged ahead
of the weed-killers. He gets scared
in the dark room at Independence Women's Clinic
where we first glimpsed his body
and a strange lady squirts goop onto Mommy's tummy,
her pooch, a shriveled melon of stretchmarks
since his birth. Mortal panorama is right.
It's a May day. Moonflowers sprout
below the lattice they once crowned. Flurries of dandelion
fluff explode across Golfview Drive. Onscreen,
the embryo appears: a white blotch among black lakes
of bladder and right ovary, just a smidgeon
of light in a dark cavity, miniature Buddha levitating
in full lotus before the void. Already apart from us,
already on a path apart from our own, it charts
a course through us. That's right:

We are waystation, conduit.
Sealed in the envelope of Lili's uterus, the letter
composes itself. Says what it wants to say.
It branches out of us, out of today's sultry heat and hearsay
of rain, leaf light and seeds catapulted,
yellow pits trailing filaments of light, cumulous white mothership
adrift, a mountain of white stone sliding right
to left, a glacier sinking below treetops.

Chiefs Cap

I wear the defeated ballcap
upon my dented head. The Chiefs
won the one and only game I've ever been to
in 2014 when my jowls dangled
with steroidal blubber. They had such a big lead
we felt safe leaving early
ahead of the masses. That's the thing
about the Chiefs, it's how much they win
that sets you up for more greatly disappointing losses.

Still, the hat Ed bought me at the game remains
the best I own. These five years
since chemo and radiation, I've had hats fade
and flop. My theory is the shorter,
snub-nosed bill of my Chiefs cap has helped it
retain the shape of my head. Its silver clasp
still secures the leather strap. Its black
is still black. Its red is still red.

June 8, Still Spring

Early morning
birdsong.

Slant light
out of the east
rubs branch
shadows deep
in the grass.

A tender breath
stirs the leaves
and a silver curtain
of rain drops.

How to be in
and not of this,
not of this
world entirely?

Down the Road

I feel good with Theo nearby.
I like the accompaniment of him playing cars
in the family room to my nonstick
pan's rainlike crackle of power greens.

I try to be flexible and follow
his lead. If he doesn't want the swing set,
I follow him down the road.

Sometimes the heat lamp of the sky
scorches my scalp, stickies my thighs
in deep blue jeans. Sometimes breezes
lift in cloud shade, raising the idea of rain.

I like to put the outside dog
in the living room crate and the inside dog
out in the rain. Afternoons
no coffee's left in the pot, I make tea.

Wild Oats

The pear tree tapers in the shape
of a candleflame, branches narrowing
to a nub of white blossoms.

Lili decides to shred the diaries
she carried home from China,
forget the time we spent apart there
because I broke up with her.

Below the bird bath, a bed of white rock
once held the shape of a swan.

Now the neck shrivels off into the side yard.
The head grows tumescent with clods,
brain tumors, bad memories.

I decide it doesn't really matter
if I take Pascal's wager because I'm not Pascal.
The pear tree tapers in the shape of a comet
at the moment of impact,

its tail held out, a knifepoint of blossoms
whereupon the sky impales itself.

The Oneironaut

I try to recall my dreams to my year-old son.
How I led you, or so it seemed,
with a stalk of stir-fried, leafy vegetable,
arugula, perhaps, God knows how you love that,

toward the parking garage. Suffice to say
he lacked a genuine interest and the manners
to feign it and, at some point,
brought down the fruit cart, scattering yellow pears,

plums and avocados all over the carpet. Last night,
when at last you came to bed, I pretended
to be asleep even as your toes iced
my calf and you basked in the warmth of my body.

Seven Years

It's the torn corner Theo likes best,
the one that snagged the wheel and shredded
in the Beijing International Airport.
He likes to finger the fray, poke through the holes,
where the blankie's most distinctly his.

What's a date after seven years of marriage?
Let's scrub the impossible stains
out of bakeware at nighttime, the brown smudges,
flecks that elude the parchment paper
no matter how well it's origamied.

Let's scrape ceramic and call that a date.
We're both too tired for sex. Theo screams in my face
while I wipe his bottom. Braced against me,
he clenches his cheeks.

Father's Day

You twist the ads that come
in the mail for doorframes and peaches
into a Father's Day bouquet.
I remove urine ring from toilet bowl.
Theo throws a tantrum over the toilet
brush dripping in its little stand.
The moment I close the door, he wants out
of the guest bedroom where he had been
so contentedly building blocks.
On our seven-year anniversary, we drive him
to the Burr Oak Woods Nature Center
where only one sticker per visit is permitted.
Alone in the bathroom, I apply mine
to the inside cover of my notebook.
You attach yours to our son's chest.
Among so many options, we both select
MAGNIFICENT MONARCHS!

Aloe Vera

Aloe Vera leaves loll like tongues
over the window ledge in the laundry room,
tongues bitten for sunburns and scalded wrists,
their blood a salve, their ooze salvation.

By its stripes we are healed, by its lisp,
its clipped tips. Amputated cactus
stumps tatter brown as burnt paper, brown
as the oak leaves padding the terracotta

pot's roots, the pin oak leaves that flood the flowerbed
every autumn, burnt pages
of the gnostic gospel of autumn when the backs
of my hands crinkle and crack like logs

cellophane packed in the flames of the firepit,
and every sunset burns the book
of my life, its leaves, its dry dinosaur skin.

Instructions for Coarsening

Wash by hand the bamboo
cutting board. Sponge the nonstick
pan with the soft side. I like
to brace the wok in the sparkly granite
slate bottom of the kitchen sink
and swirl suds from the semipermeable
blue membrane of the sponge.

Walking the boy before bed, I hold him
in the shade of my own
shadow. The bald light slicing
low along Golfview Drive razor-burns
my cheeks. Daily gloved in foam,
my hands coarsen. Lili's hands are coarser still.

Hard to admit there are evenings
I prefer kitchen work to bedtime procedure,
the calming of water and silent,
inanimate objects: quartz countertop,
lacquered butcher block, sunset-dusted
window panes, turmeric.

Cravings

Nights you sigh and moan
because you're hungry I really have
no patience for. Still, I peel
potato over the trash can. Wet swaths
of brown skin hang from the white
plastic lining. I rotate
in my palsied left, clearing my fingers
from the slip while maintaining
a firm hold on the spud
that hovers over a landfill of egg shells,
balled up napkins, banana peels.

Once I have it down to a few
spots of stubborn skin, I halve
the uneven lump, then quarter hemispheres.
Come up from the study and I scissor
slices of bacon into bits, insinuate
discs of zucchini into the sizzle
and snap of the skillet. Lastly leaves
of cabbage I tear by hand.

You lean over the quartz countertop
in your camo bathrobe, picking out pieces
with chopsticks and turning them
over in turmeric, red pepper and salt.

You're pregnant and deserve
to be ravenous. I ask for less, for half
the steak in the skillet. Half is not enough
for you. One and a half is too much.
Yet you finish it, sitting alone
at the butcher block,
and go out for a cup of Black Forest
after Theo's asleep.

What am I to do in the face of such relentless need,
the restlessness of your cravings,
when I'm just trying to watch my movie
and not worry about the sensations
in my head, whether right side
or left, tumor or caffeine,
O please be caffeine. How petty
it is to complain.

Memory Gaps

Like Cindy who has no memory
of the year her family
exploded with the propane tank
in the trunk, Lili remembers
little of the bombshell day
of my diagnosis, how I wanted
no one near me, not even her,
and ate an all-beef polish alone
in the Costco cafeteria. Now,
when I wait with her engine running
in the parking lot of HOBBY LOBBY,
I pass our son in the car seat
a loaded bubble wand, rainbow
membrane stretched like a drumhead
ready to balloon around his
baby breath. He pops it
into his mouth. (So much
for that idea.) When I press
the refrigerator for ice, cubes
hit the rim of my Contigo
and scatter fire over tile floor.
I have yet to address the WWF
sticker attached to the back
corner of my study door, though
others must have tried
because its entire margin is tattered
white, leaving only the spray-tanned torso
and one tauntingly extended arm.

The Steamin' Bean

I step onto my son's stool. Reach the top shelf
mugs and replace them with bottom
shelf mugs. Reach the back shelf mugs and replace
them with front shelf mugs. The pleasure
I take in this is similar to the pleasure I take in
loading dirty forks and spoons in the rearmost compartment
of the flatware rack and working my way
forward. Lots of people online call their brain tumors
the beast or the monster. Mine's had a lot
of positive effects. Like put up or shut up.
Buckle down and have kids. A plain white mug
in the top back corner is labeled The Steamin' Bean
after a coffeeshop that tanked in the parking lot
of Blue Springs 8 Theatre. Christmas break,
2009: *Avatar*. Every morning, I drove to have a coffee
and chat online with the nocturnal
woman I would marry.

IKEA

Some movies are endlessly quotable
like *The Princess Bride*
or *Groundhog Day*. Some references
are so ingrained I can't recall
where they come from. In the showroom,

I babble to my wife and son. Describe
a checkered lampshade as *retro*. A moment later,
I hear the word *retro* echoed back to me
in a stranger's language. In passing,
I hear it again, my word

minimalistic. I feel powerful,
a puppet master, a maker of persons.
I name my son Theodore and a first
cousin names her son the same.
I name my daughter Naomi, sit back and wait.

White Petals

This morning's sky macabre,
clouds shade the lawn.

White petals flurry
between the ornamental pear

and cedar pickets. Each one
with its own twirl, its own unique

flourish a result of the crinkle, size
and weight with which it's made

partnered to the breeze that coaxes it
into freefall. Who am I

that one should alight
upon the last pages of my tired notebook?

A morning much like this one,
four years ago, rides out of me:

my little sister Jessie driving me home
from my bi-weekly blood draw,

now married mother of two, my baby
sister steering me home

in the butterfly needles
of spring rain, her brother's arm crook

wrapped, his blotted cotton ball
the lump in her throat.

Who am I to have received such love,
who are any of us, indeed?

Paradise

I live in the garden.
Garden's in the name of my neighborhood:
Country Club Gardens. My neighbors
plant flowers and flowering
trees. There are birds
here: robins and sparrows mostly,
then crows, always
crows. We hope for hummingbirds
and in that hope hang a feeder
among the tomato cages in the garden
in which I live. I like to recycle
cardboard and plastic. I tell myself
even if the companies are lying
to me and filling the land with my trash,
I am not wrong for believing.
The companies are wrong for lying
and that's on them. Here,
in Eden, I have never golfed but every
morning golfers unsheathe
shining silver clubs. My boy and I admire them
from the roped off rock bed.

Going to the Mayo Clinic

Not in Arizona, Florida
or Minnesota, I sit out on my own back patio

for the moment, but who's to say what Tuesday's
results might be,

what cross-country flights might follow?

All I know is this morning
clouds are dragging sooty sleeves

out of the west. A tantrum broods
north of Blue Springs,

an arm crook needle bruised with scar
tissue: me during chemo.

Would you minister to the part of me that is always aching,
it is told so often it is going to die, it has forgotten
it's still alive?

I would stand where sunrise cuts my shadow clean
over soggy grass and sink
my feet in.

Coat Hook

I flick the cicada
latched to the garage door
frame with a few broom straws.
The army green airman
sputters to life and motors away
through dark morning air.
As much as I love my life, it can be saddening
to wake up in the morning: I knew a man
who would smile at himself
a full five minutes in the bathroom mirror,
every morning. Imagine:
teeth bared, deadlocked in your own stare,
your own wrinkled eyes, a full five.
In the bathroom, my eyes land,
for the first time, on a golden coat hook
screwed into the ceiling. Might as well
have been an attic ladder door.
On the tile floor, Lili's hairs twirl together
into these knots among blade
tips of grass my little brother cuts for a living.
No matter the forecast, he can convince
himself the storm clouds are going to pass
east of us or west. Seized by some
strange whimsy, I hang the utility lighter
by its trigger guard.

Apple Cider Vinegar

Where the moonflowers have engulfed the lattice that was erected to support the heads of their violet blossoms, I swat the black-and-white striped mosquito, white welt on freckled forearm, sun still hot in the sun, chill as a blade in the shade. From the garbage can corner of the kitchen floor Theo forages a morsel of something lost or thrown away. Lili cups his pooched cheeks and squeezes. Mariah refills the dish drowning fruit flies in apple cider vinegar. Passes her cold along to Grandma. The ceramic bird house bus Barb ends by giving to Theo because of his frequent visits, his unstoppable trespasses, for another interval floated in the wisteria arbor, bungeed to timberbeam, before I restored it to his grasp, sudsing out the porthole in the sink, something lost or thrown away, early autumn wind in the branches, stirrings, strings of the invisible harpsichord, the cricket cabaret. Holiness is this, meeting my sister at Panera for coffee as friends, an old teacher at Starbucks as friends. Being happy with this gift of some autumn breath. How nothing as a given implies the givenness of all things.

NOTES:

"Invocation of a Black Orb-Weaver" is a response to Bashō's injunction:

In composing hokku, there are two ways: becoming and making. When a poet who has always been assiduous in the pursuit of his aim applies himself to an external object, the color of his mind naturally becomes the poem.

The Essential Haiku: Versions of Bashō, Buson, and Issa. HarperCollins, 1994.

The epigraph to "Perceiving Mystery" comes from Stephen Addiss and Stanley Lombardo's translation of the *Tao Te Ching.* Hackett Publishing Company, 1993.

"What's Still" is a response to Bashō's distinction:

What's still has changeless form. Moving things change, and because we cannot put a stop to time, it continues unarrested. To stop a thing would be to halve a sight or sound in our heart.

The Essential Haiku: Versions of Bashō, Buson, and Issa. HarperCollins, 1994.

"New Member" is a response to a post on the Facebook group "GBM SURVIVORS TO THIVERS!"

"Newborn Panorama" began as a reply to Jordan Stempleman's blurb of my second collection *Father Me Again.*

Cameron Morse was diagnosed with a glioblastoma in 2014. With a 14.6 month life expectancy, he entered the Creative Writing Program at the University of Missouri—Kansas City and, in 2018, graduated with an M.F.A. His poems have been published in numerous magazines, including *New Letters, Bridge Eight, Portland Review* and *South Dakota Review*. His first poetry collection, *Fall Risk,* won Glass Lyre Press's 2018 Best Book Award. His subsequent collections are *Father Me Again* (Spartan Press, 2018), *Coming Home with Cancer* (Blue Lyra Press, 2019) and *Terminal Destination* (Spartan Press, 2019). He lives with his wife Lili and their two children in Blue Springs, Missouri, where he serves as poetry editor for *Harbor Review.*

www.ingramcontent.com/pod-product-compliance
Lightning Source LLC
Chambersburg PA
CBHW030347100526
44592CB00010B/862